SPORTS WOMEN LEGENDS ALPHABET

Words by Robin Feiner

Aa

is for Michelle   kers.
With her commanding presence
on and off the field, this
trailblazing soccer legend is
one of only two women named
in the FIFA 100. She was also
awarded the Golden Boot for
her top-scoring success in the
1991 World Cup.

B is for Bonnie **B**lair.
This world-record-holding speed skater was the youngest child in a large family of speed skaters. On the day she was born, the rest of her family was out competing! Blair is the most decorated woman in Winter Olympic Games history.

C is for Nadia **C**omăneci. This wunderkind was the first to ever score a perfect 10 in an Olympic gymnastics event. She went on to achieve six more perfect scores, and she was only 15 years old! Comăneci was inducted into the Gymnastics Hall of Fame in 1993.

D is for Danica Patrick.
An early interest in go-karting led to this motorsport legend beating the boys at their own game. She is the only woman to win an IndyCar Series race, and the most successful woman in open-wheel racing history!

E is for Teresa **E**dwards. As a child, this basketball virtuoso spent hours shooting baskets at trash cans. When her mom told her not to try out for her middle-school team, she didn't listen. Instead, she went on to win four Olympic gold medals!

Ff

F is for **F**lorence Griffith Joyner. As a child, 'Flo-Jo' improved her speed by chasing jackrabbits. As an adult, she set a world record for the 100m sprint that still stands today. Sporting her long nails and flashy style, she earned herself the title of 'the fastest woman on earth.'

G is for Steffi Graf.
With her athletic ability
and aggressive game at the
baseline, Graf is credited with
inventing the modern style.
As well as winning 22 Grand
Slam titles, Germany's golden
girl made history as the first
and only winner of a Golden
Grand Slam. Wunderbar!

H is for Mia **H**amm. With her impressive goal-scoring record, this soccer icon gives today's most popular male players a run for their money. At 15, she became the youngest member to join a U.S. team, and has scored a whopping 158 goals in international competition!

is for Ila Borders.
This trailblazing left-handed
pitcher was the first woman to
ever open a men's professional
baseball game, and the first to
receive a baseball scholarship
to play men's college baseball.
Her curve ball was a force to
be reckoned with!

J is for Jackie **J**oyner-Kersee. Just five points short of a gold medal at her first Olympic Games in 1984, this track and field legend returned with a vengeance, becoming the first athlete to score 7,000 points in the heptathlon! She is considered the greatest female athlete of all time.

K is for Billie Jean **K**ing. Small, speedy and aggressive, this outspoken revolutionary refused to conform from the get-go, appearing in a junior group photo wearing shorts instead of a skirt. With 39 major titles to her name, she fought for and won gender equality for women in tennis.

L is for Lisa Leslie.
A natural left-hander, this determined basketball legend taught herself to play right-handed in high school. Her ambidexterity became a distinct advantage — she won four Olympic golds and was the first player to 'dunk' in a WNBA match.

Mm

M is for **M**artina Navratilova. She was hitting a tennis ball against a concrete wall in Prague at the age of four, and had won the Czechoslovakian national tennis title by age 15. Including doubles, she won more Grand Slam titles than any other player in history!

N is for **N**ancy Lopez. At a time when interest in women's golf was waning, this charismatic golfing prodigy burst onto the scene and took the game to peak popularity. She won so many consecutive tournaments that everyone knew her simply as 'Nancy.'

Oo

O is for Margo Oberg.
This surfing legend won her first competition at 11, and her first title at 15, but then after a disappointing loss in the 1970 World Contest, she retired to finish high school. Oberg made a comeback in 1975 and became the first professional female surfer in history!

P is for Natalia **P**artyka. Being born without a right hand and forearm didn't stop her from winning gold at both able-bodied and Paralympic table tennis competitions! At 11 years of age, she became the youngest Paralympian in history.

Q is for **Q**ueen of the Waves, Gertrude Ederle. Proving everyone wrong and shattering the gender stereotypes of the time, she became the first woman to swim across the English Channel in 1926! She said afterwards, "I knew it could be done, it had to be done, and I did it." Legendary!

Rr

R is for Ronda **R**ousey.
Giving new meaning to the
phrase 'fight like a girl,' this
Olympic judo champ turned
her historic bronze medal win
into a lucrative Mixed Martial
Arts career. She went on
to become the first female
champion in UFC history.

S is for **S**erena Williams. She first picked up a tennis racket at the tender age of three. Then decades later, with her sister Venus, she ushered in a new era of power in women's tennis. Serena holds the most Grand Slam titles of any active player, and was ranked No. 1 eight times in 15 years.

Tt

T is for **T**racy Caulkins. This Swimming Hall of Famer had hyperextended knees that gave her a powerful dolphin-like kick. Over the course of her career, she excelled in every stroke, set 66 world and U.S. records, and held 48 titles in all!

U is for **U**rsula Hayden. This professional wrestler and actress found fame as 'Babe' on the influential 80s TV show, 'Gorgeous Ladies of Wrestling' (GLOW). She later bought the franchise, and proved that women's wrestling can be just as lucrative as men's. Smackdown!

V is for Lindsey **V**onn.
For three consecutive years,
this legendary speed skier
was an Olympic gold medallist
and World Cup champion. One
of only six women to have
won World Cup races in all five
disciplines of the sport, Vonn
has a record-breaking 82
World Cup victories.

W is for Wilma Rudolph. After contracting polio as a child, this international track and field star was told she would never walk again, but she chose not to believe it. With three Olympic gold medals and three world record titles, Wilma went on to become 'the fastest woman in the world.'

X is for **X**-treme Kelly Clark. This trailblazing snowboarder was the first woman to land a front-side 1080 — that's three full revolutions! She is the most dominant competitive snowboarder in history, male or female. What a legend!

Y is for Yu Chui Yee.
This talented Paralympian began her sporting career as a swimmer then switched to wheelchair fencing. She is the first athlete to have won four gold medals in fencing, and was her team's flag bearer at the 2016 Paralympic Games opening ceremony.

Z is for Babe Didrikson **Z**aharias. Born in 1911, this legend excelled in basketball, golf, and track and field. Winning three medals at the 1932 Olympic Games, her medal tally was only hindered by the now out-dated rule that prevented women from competing in more than three Olympic events.

The ever-expanding legendary library

EXPLORE THESE LEGENDARY ALPHABETS & MORE AT WWW.ALPHABETLEGENDS.COM

SPORTSWOMEN LEGENDS ALPHABET
www.alphabetlegends.com

Published by Alphabet Legends Pty Ltd in 2019
Created by Beck Feiner
Copyright © Alphabet Legends Pty Ltd 2019

9 780648 506317

Printed and bound in China.